THE CHOLESTERO

Excess cholesterol in t[...]
causes of heart trouble [...]
be controlled. These d[...] [...]onstrate
how you can cut down on harmful, high-cholesterol
ingredients without feeling deprived.

By the same author
ARTHRITIS: Help In Your Own Hands
DIETS TO HELP ARTHRITIS
With Henry Rowsell
A MODERN BEE HERBAL

THE CHOLESTEROL CONTROL COOKBOOK

Dozens of Recipes for a Healthy Heart

by

HELEN B. MacFARLANE

NATURE'S WAY

THORSONS PUBLISHERS LIMITED
Wellingborough, Northamptonshire

First published 1977
Second Impression 1978

ISBN 0 7225 0382 2

Photoset by
Specialised Offset Services Limited, Liverpool
and printed in Great Britian by
Weatherby Woolnough Ltd.,
Sanders Road, Wellingborough, Northamptonshire.

CONTENTS

The state of the 'science' of nutrition today is not unlike that of Humpty Dumpty. It, like Humpty Dumpty, and quite as unwittingly, has fragmented itself into separate pieces, so that the whole has become lost and no one knows how to put it together again.

ACKNOWLEDGEMENT

Sincere thanks are expressed to *Prevention* for permission to include in this book some recipes previously published in their magazine.

INTRODUCTION

Balance, variety of foods and small or moderate, rather than large, helpings provide the key to cholesterol control as well as to many of our chronic or acute disabilities. My own experience and the reading of up-to-date scientific literature on dietary trends quite convinces me of the truth of this statement. It is known that the body can cope better with four to five small meals in a day (particularly in the case of middle-aged or elderly people) than with two or three large ones, and that a nutritious and well balanced breakfast can make all the difference between good health and the 'half' health which is such a common manifestation today.

There has been much publicity in the media and elsewhere about the necessity for cholesterol control, but this is a very complex subject. Individuals vary greatly in their ability to cope with foods containing cholesterol, and also in their needs for this fatty substance – for the body *does* need it. It is present in all animal products and this is where the complications set in.

We hear about saturated fats and unsaturated fats, about mono-unsaturated fats and polyunsaturated fats, about animal fats and vegetable fats and oils, about those which are hydrogenated and those which are unhydrogenated. If we are concerned about the amounts of excess cholesterol which may build up in veins and arteries from day to day, causing blockages, how are we to unscramble all this information and at the same time keep up a balanced way of eating without each meal becoming a veritable nightmare?

On a practical level, it seems best to boil it all down to a few facts in line with present knowledge and, rather than count calories or attempt to keep track of amounts of cholesterol-producing foods in each meal, to work towards variety and, above all, to avoid excessive quantities of any one food at a time. It would also be advisable, for instance, not to put large daubs of margarine (of any variety), butter, or other fatty substances on cooked vegetables from day to day, as this could build up cholesterol which might react unfavourably with other foods, particularly if not combined with vitamin E. Minute amounts on vegetables are adequate and equally palatable. This advise also applies to many other foods in which fats are used, including sauces and salad dressings.

For the purpose of this book the reader should be aware, however, of the various types of fat, so as to be able to decipher what is conveyed on the labels of foods such as margarine and vegetable oils and to be aware of the quality of protein provided by meat, fish, nuts, beans, insofar as their fat content is concerned.

Generally speaking, a saturated fat, which is supposed to be the chief villain in the cholesterol story, is a fat which hardens at room temperature.

This is found particularly in beef because of present day methods of production, and it is suggested that the leanest parts of the animal are the healthiest for human consumption. Organ meats, egg yolks, butter, cream, whole milk and cheeses are also high in cholesterol, but in their natural states they also contain substances which combine with cholesterol and help the body to assimilate it. Small quantities of any of these (though not eaten every day) should not be harmful if common sense is used.

Unsaturated fat is generally accepted as a fat which is liquid at room temperature, in contrast to saturated fat which is hard and set at room temperature. The unsaturated fat is divided into two types, mono-unsaturated and polyunsaturated. The effect of the mono-unsaturated fats has been found to be neutral so far as raising or lowering the level of cholesterol in the blood is concerned. They are present mainly in nuts, in olive and peanut oils.

Polyunsaturated fat, on the other hand, has a tendency to lower the cholesterol level in the blood and to help the body to eliminate excess cholesterol, particularly if it is newly formed. This useful fat is found for the most part in oils of vegetable origin, such as safflower, sunflower, corn or cotton seed. Yet there are snags and dangers even in this.

Behind these effects lies the same old story of processed foods. In the raw state most fats and oils that are high in polyunsaturated fatty acids also contain enough natural antioxidants to keep the oils from combining with oxygen in the bloodstream, thus forming poisonous peroxides, but it is now known that during heating the antioxidants in such oils are destroyed. Using oil or margarine for frying is best avoided, and this is particularly so in cases where the same oil is frequently reheated, as in deep frying. Moreover, most margarines are so highly processed that all the protective vitamin E has disappeared.

Many margarines do contain the polyunsaturated oils which are so beneficial in their natural state, but here again man has stepped in. They are processed not only to the extent that many of their essential nutrients are lost, but are also put through a further process known as hydrogenation. This adds 'shelf life' to the oils and prevents them from going rancid, but at the same time it turns them for the most part into mono-unsaturated or saturated fats. Often there is no indication of this on the label.

Though not apparently having any direct connection with the build-up of excess cholesterol, salt in excess is known to play havoc with the delicately balanced machinery of the body. It has been established that this can be one of the chief underlying causes of high blood pressure and other related diseases. Many people may not be aware that salt has already been added to most of the ordinary foods they consume, particulary breakfast cereals and other ready-to-eat processed foods. This is particularly dangerous, because potassium is needed to neutralize the effects of over-consumption of sodium. Potassium is found in the natural, whole grains, such as unprocessed oats.

Despite the publicity directed against it, the body needs cholesterol to perform various valuable functions – in fact the body manufactures cholesterol itself. It is necessary for the formation of vitamin D, the sex and adrenal hormones, and the bile salts so important in the digestion of fats. The reason why the cholesterol the body manufactures does not collect in the arteries is that each time cholesterol occurs in the natural state, through food or otherwise, it is accompanied by lecithin (see *Supplements*). It is the cholesterol received from processed foods which is a major cause of trouble, partly through hydrogenated fats from which the lecithin has been removed. Those who habitually eat large quantities of animal and hydrogenated fats and little in the way of raw nuts, avocados or seeds are likely to be short of this essential substance, unless they take lecithin in the form of capsules or include it in their diet. Otherwise they are preparing the ground for the formation of excess cholesterol in their veins and arteries.

Some researchers in Europe are beginning to suspect that, although cholesterol deposits on the walls of the arteries are symptomatic of cardio-vascular disease, cholesterol itself is not the cause. The trouble lies in a general inability to handle cholesterol. The fact is emerging from articles in the popular press and elsewhere that many people, such as the North American Eskimo and some of the tribes of Northern Siberia, habitually consume large quantities of cholesterol-rich foods yet heart disease is practically unknown among them – so long as they refrain from adopting 'civilized' ways of eating. When white sugar, white flour, excess table salt, processed and tinned foods are brought into their lives their health immediately begins to deteriorate and they become susceptible to all the diseases and weaknesses so prevalent in the 'advanced' countries of the world.

In Western society, apart from the tendency to overeat (and usually of the wrong foods), we have to face the fact that we have long been exposed to large doses of nitrates and other fertilizers, as well as pesticides of all kinds. The nervous and emotional stresses to which so many are prone today and many other debilitating hazards also take their toll. Any of these can so weaken the defences of the body that the inevitable effect is a breakdown of some sort, and an inability to handle cholesterol could be the result in certain susceptible people.

So it is that the most advanced research seems to point out that it is these external hazards, along with our own individual way of life, particularly our eating habits, which lead to the build-up of cholesterol with its devastating effects. And white sugar and white flour products, along with other processed and devitalized foods, seem to be the chief villains of the piece.

Much has been written by Dr John Yudkin, Professor of Nutrition at London University, and other investigators, about the disastrous effects on the heart and other organs of the over-consumption of sugar. In one study Dr Yudkin found that patients hospitalized for a heart attack or other cardiovascular problems had been consuming twice as much sugar as a healthy control group. Numerous experiments have shown that dietary sugar can dangerously raise serum cholesterol and triglyceride levels, just as in certain cases can dietary fat.

It must be stressed again that more and more evidence is coming to the fore which cites white sugar as a most serious menace to the health of all, including babies and children. When consumed in the quantities so usual amongst the general population today, it can lead to a gradual and potentially dangerous deterioration in health. A body which is overloaded with this devitalized chemical substance is in no condition to cope with germs, 'viruses', a build-up of cholesterol, or any other disease-producing factor. Nor can it cope with the complex drugs prescribed by so many doctors to dampen down symptoms. This is the way to the deterioration of health.

Coronary thrombosis is now the major cause of heart attack deaths. It takes the lives of over a million people a year in the United States alone, yet the disease was unknown before 1900. It may be interesting to note, too, that it was about this time millers began to refine flour to greater and greater degrees, thus effectively removing all the vitamin E and many other protective and nutritive substances.

The main fact which seems to emerge from the many investigations which have taken place to try to determine the workings of the body and the best way of feeding it is that the interactions of one food with another are still impossible to gauge. But one thing is known – once a food is torn apart in the processing it is quite impossible to replace all the elements which have been lost. We simply do not know what many of them are.

It does seem fairly certain, in view of the confused state of nutritional science today, that the only way an individual can protect himself is to stick to a plain, well-balanced diet, using as many unprocessed foods as possible. This was driven home recently by scientists connected with the World Health Organization who had this to say: 'As many as nine out of ten cancers might be prevented by changing the way we live.' And I am sure that this statement could be applied equally well to many of our other serious complaints, including the build-up of cholesterol.

It is not easy to change a way of life, nor a way of eating, but the diets and recipes suggested in this book can be easily followed or adapted to suit people of any age and in any circumstances. What is needed is a certain amount of care and thought, so that a good balance of ordinary food is consumed from day to day. Variety is the key, with emphasis on quality rather than on quantity.

From his own insight and his experience of treating and helping people over many years, Dr Bircher-Benner wrote: 'To concern oneself about one's body or one's nutrition is of no avail unless a new awakening, a new awareness of one's inner forces results. The wonders of the spirit remain a closed book to those who constantly disregard the laws of nutrition. The force and depth of inner experience depend on nutrition to an inconceivable extent.'

WEIGHTS AND MEASURES

Most of the recipes in this book are based on American measurements, as I find them convenient and time-saving compared with the laborious business of weighing everything out. However, for the purposes of those who prefer to use scales some comparative measurements are given below:

English	American	Fluid Ounces
1 teaspoonful	1¼ teaspoonsful	1/6 to 1/3
1 dessertspoonful		½
1 tablespoonful	1¼ tablespoonsful	1 to 2
1 teacupful		about 7 oz. (1/3 pint)
	1 measuring cup	8 oz. (½ pint)

Above weights apply to liquid measurements only. In dry, measurements whether the spoon or cup is 'level,' 'heaped,' 'rounded,' etc., must also affect quantity. Fortunately, in a kitchen some leeway is permitted and with experience one finds these measurements quick and effective. Perhaps it might be dubbed 'green thumb' rather than scientific cooking.

Standard measuring cups, dividing into quarters, thirds, etc., are now available in many ironmongers or other shops.

	One measuring Cup	One Teacup
Dried beans	4 oz.	
Dried bread crumbs	2 oz.	
Butter or margarine (2 tablespoonsful 1 oz.)	8 oz.	
Dates (chopped)	8 oz.	
Figs	8 oz.	
Flour	4 oz.	$2\frac{1}{2}$ oz.
Meat (chopped)	8 oz.	
Nuts (chopped)	8 oz.	
Oats	4 oz.	$2\frac{1}{2}$ oz.
Raisins, Currants	8 oz.	5 oz.
Sugar, brown	$2\frac{1}{2}$ measuring cups to 1 pound	

(An average breakfast cup is approximately the size of a standard measuring cup.)

OVEN TEMPERATURES

Very slow	250°F.	Moderately hot	375-400°F.
Slow	300°F.	Fairly hot	425°F.
Moderately slow	325°F.	Hot	450°F.
Moderate	350°F.	Very hot	475-500°F.

Without a thermometer, the following tests are fairly reliable:

Moderate oven: A piece of white paper should brown in two minutes.

Hot oven: A piece of white paper should brown in $1\frac{1}{2}$ minutes.

Gas cookers (Regulo)

$\frac{1}{4}$ equals 240°F.	5 equals 380°F.
$\frac{1}{2}$ equals 265°F.	6 equals 400°F.
1 equals 290°F.	7 equals 425°F.
2 equals 310°F.	8 equals 445°F.
3 equals 335°F.	9 equals 470°F.
4 equals 355°F.	

BREAKFAST DISHES

In 1951 Jacobus Rinse, Ph.D., suffered an attack of angina due to atherosclerosis and was warned by his doctor that he had ten years to live 'if all physical exercise was avoided'. Instead of giving up a normal life and abiding by this dictum, Dr Rinse, a consulting chemist, over a period of years studied the needs of the body and came up with the hypothesis that the foods he ate must contain everything in adequate quantities and should be varied as much as possible.

His famous breakfast was one result of this study and it is in use all over the world. Dr Rinse, now a hale and hearty septuagenarian, found his diet not only helped his ailing heart but freed him from colds, flu, arthritis, bursitis and backache. He cites other cases where heart conditions have been helped by his diet, with its special emphasis on lecithin and vitamin E.

Dr Rinse's Breakfast
A tablespoonful each of soya lecithin granules, debittered yeast and raw wheat germ, 1 teaspoonful of bone meal (from a health store). The bone meal is important because the calcium in it is needed to

balance the phosphorus in the lecithin.

To 2 tablespoonsful of this mixture are added 1 tablespoonful of dark brown or raw sugar, and 1 tablespoonful of safflower or soyabean oil. This is dissolved in milk and yogurt is added. Also add cold or hot cereal (to provide calories) and raisins or other fruit if desired.

For severe cases of atherosclerosis he suggests doubling the quantity of lecithin and using daily 500 mg of vitamin C, along with 100 i.u. of vitamin E, and one multivitamin-mineral tablet.

Granola

$1\frac{1}{2}$ cups rolled oats
$\frac{1}{2}$ cup rolled rye
$\frac{1}{2}$ cup unprocessed bran
2 tablespoonsful honey
$\frac{1}{4}$ cup water
$\frac{1}{2}$ cup ground almonds
$\frac{1}{2}$ cup sunflower seeds
$\frac{1}{2}$ cup unsweetened coconut
2 tablespoonsful oil

Combine above ingredients, stirring until grains and nuts are well coated. Pour mixture into a large shallow baking pan which has been slightly oiled and toast in a slow oven for $1\frac{1}{2}$ hours, stirring occasionally or until mixture is dry, lightly browned and crisp. After cooling store in a glass jar in the refrigerator.

Muesli

A tablespoonful or two of 'quick' (precooked) dry oats, with stewed figs, prunes, apricots, and/or soaked sultanas, a dessertspoonful of soya flour or soya splits (see *Soya*). Wheat germ and bran flakes can also be added.

Shredded wheat, whole meal bread, bran breakfast foods and other non-refined foods are better than those which have lost much of their food value by processing.

Bircher-Benner Muesli: – Basic Recipe

(N.B. Rolled oats or oatmeal must be soaked for 12 hours before being used in this recipe – unless quick-cooking).

1 level tablespoonful rolled oats (or 1 dessertspoonful medium oatmeal) soaked for 12 hours in 3 tablespoonsful water.
1 tablespoonful lemon juice
1 tablespoonful evaporated skim milk
1 large apple
1 tablespoonful grated hazelnuts or almonds

Mix lemon juice and milk to a smooth cream, then add to oats, stirring thoroughly. Wash and wipe apple, remove top, stalk and any blemishes. Grate apple into mixture, stirring frequently to prevent discolouring. Sprinkle nuts over the finished dish and serve immediately.

The cereal need not always consist of rolled oats or oatmeal. Soaked, fresh whole wheat grains, soya flakes, millet flakes, wheat germ, germinated wheat or other sprouts may be used. More nutritious than dry cereals or 'quick' oats are the kinds which take 5 minutes or more to cook, particularly steel cut oats. Ordinary Scottish oats undergo some processing, but luckily when they are milled the bran and germ do remain. Whole grain cereals made from toasted wheat, with wheat germ added are also good. Cereals such as cream of wheat and cream of rice are too refined to be of much value nutritionally.

Wheat germ, brewer's yeast or yogurt added to

cooked, unrefined cereals will make a complete protein dish. Sunflower seeds, sesame seeds or nuts can also be added.

Modern research has shown that cereals retain more of their nutritional value when cooked only 5-15 minutes, rather than for hours as was formerly thought necessary.

SOUPS

Beef Stock
Have the bones broken small, cut meat into small cubes. If meat is raw brown it in a little vegetable oil in a frying pan with sliced onions. Cover meat and bones with water, soak for 1 hour, then simmer for 4 hours, or until the meat is soft. When stock is cold remove fat which has solidified on the surface. Remove meat and bones. Boil up daily for better keeping.

Removing Fat from Soups
If fat is difficult to remove draw a piece of blotting paper, or unglazed paper dipped in cold water, across the top.

To Clarify Stock
Stir into stock to be cleared the whites and crushed shells of as many eggs as there are quarts (litres) of stock. Heat and stir until it has boiled for 2 minutes. Then add $\frac{1}{4}$ cup of cold water for each quart of stock. Keep stock hot, not boiling or simmering, for 20 minutes. Pour through a fine strainer with muslin laid over it.

Veal or White Stock

Use a knuckle of veal with bones broken fairly small. Heat slowly in 4 quarts of water, less if knuckle is a small one. Simmer 4 hours, skimming frequently; add 1 stalk celery, 1 onion, 1 bay leaf, 1 dessert-spoonful sea salt. Simmer 1 hour longer. This could jell when cold, when the fat can be removed. It can also be cleared as above, if desired.

Vegetable Stock

Vegetables may be varied according to season and availability.

1 tablespoonful vegetable oil
1 onion
2 medium carrots, a small parsnip, or a little swede
1 small cup shredded or diced celery or celeriac
cabbage, beet leaves or other green vegetables
6-8 pints ($3\frac{1}{2}$-$4\frac{1}{2}$ litres) cold water
basil, lovage, or other fresh or dried herbs
$\frac{1}{2}$ bay leaf
salt and a little pepper

Skin the onion, halve it and brown cut surface in the oil. Add the sliced vegetables to the onion and stew gently for $\frac{1}{4}$ hour in a covered saucepan. Add cold water, simmer for 2 hours. Season.

Cream Soups

These can be made by pressing cooked vegetables through a sieve, and adding to them a hot, thin white sauce. Bring mixture to the boil, remove from heat and whisk or beat. Alternatively, add milk to the sieved vegetables and heat up.

Lentil Cream Soup

$\frac{1}{2}$ cup lentils
$\frac{1}{2}$ pint (275 ml) skim milk
1 quart (1 litre) stock or water
1 small onion
1 small carrot

Soak lentils overnight. Add to water or stock and bring to the boil. Add vegetables and allow to simmer for about 2 hours. Rub through sieve, return to saucepan and add scalded milk.

Lentil Soup

$\frac{1}{2}$ cup lentils
$\frac{1}{2}$ cup barley
2 pints (1 litre) water
1 small piece turnip
1 carrot
cabbage, onion and other available vegetables

Wash lentils. Prepare other vegetables, cutting them into small pieces. Add all ingredients to the water, season to taste, and simmer for approximately 3 hours.

Haricot or Butter Bean Soup

$\frac{1}{2}$ lb (225 g) beans
2 pints (1 litre) vegetable stock
3 small onions
1 cup chopped turnip or swede
seasoning

Beans should be soaked overnight, then added, with liquor, to vegetable stock. Add chopped onions and simmer until beans are soft. Pass through sieve, and reheat before serving.

Celery Soup

1 head celery
1¼ pints (700 ml) stock
1 pint (550 ml) milk
1 level tablespoonful plain wholemeal flour
seasoning

Prepare celery, removing only the large green leaves. Chop it into small pieces and add to the stock. Bring to the boil and simmer for about 1 hour. Season with a little sea salt. Rub through a sieve or blend to a purée in an electric liquidizer. Mix flour with the cold milk. Bring stock and celery purée to boil, pour over flour and cold milk. Return to saucepan and cook on low heat, stirring, for about 5 minutes. Garnish with parsley or watercress.

Artichoke Soup

1½ lb (675 g) Jerusalem artichokes
1 onion or a few green leek tops, chopped
1½ pints (825 ml) vegetable stock
¼ pint (150 ml) skim milk

Scrub artichokes, then chop into small pieces or grate. Cook artichokes and onion or leek tops in the stock until soft. Add milk, reheat and serve. Season to taste.

Clear Leek Soup

This soup can be made in 15-20 minutes. Wash and cut two leeks very finely. Bring to boil in 1 pint (550 ml) water or stock and simmer for 10-15 minutes. Season.

Leek and Oatmeal Soup

Use the green tops of leeks, washed and cut into

small pieces. Allow $1\frac{1}{2}$ pints (825 ml) of water or stock to 1 lb (450 g) of the leek tops. Bring to boil and sprinkle in 2 level tablespoonsful medium oatmeal. Cook slowly for about 1 hour, stirring occasionally. A tablespoonful of chopped parsley may be added just before serving.

Clear Rice Soup
1 tablespoonful vegetable oil
1 small onion, chopped
1 small carrot
piece of celery or celeriac
1 small leek
3 tablespoonsful rice
4 pints ($2\frac{1}{4}$ litres) vegetable stock
chives, seasoning

Chop all vegetables finely and brown them in the oil. Add rice and stock and cook for about 20 minutes. Add chives and seasoning.

Tomato Cream Soup
1 pint sieved tomato pulp (fresh or tinned)
$\frac{1}{2}$ pint (275 ml) skim milk
2 tablespoonsful very finely chopped or grated onion
2 tablespoonsful grated horseradish or horseradish sauce

Put vegetables into saucepan, add milk and heat, being very careful not to let the soup boil.

Pea Soup
$1\frac{1}{2}$ cups dried split peas
2 pints (1 litre) water
$\frac{1}{4}$ pint (150 ml) skim milk
1 large onion
1 small carrot
small piece of turnip
seasoning

Wash peas and soak overnight. Cut vegetables finely.
Put all into saucepan, including water in which peas
are soaked. Add water and seasoning. Simmer gently
for about 2 hours. (If preferred the soup may be
passed through a sieve before adding the milk.) Add
milk, reheat, and serve.

Quick Carrot Soup
Scrub carrots. Grate or cut into narrow strips. Add to
hot stock and cook until they are soft, which should
be in about 15 minutes.

FISH

To Skin A Fish
Cut a narrow strip along the backbone with a sharp knife, removing the fin on the back. Then run the knife up through and under the bony part of the gills, peeling the skin off, backwards towards the tail. Peel off the skin from the other side in the same manner.

Steamed Fish
Wash, scale, and otherwise prepare fish. Cover with greaseproof paper and place in the steamer. About 10 minutes per pound is required.

Thin fillets may be cooked between two plates in a little milk.

When cooked the fish may be served with a garnish of parsley, lemon or tomatoes, or with a sauce, made with whole wheat flour.

Boiled Fish
Only enough water is required to cover the fish. Cooking time will be 5-10 minutes per pound, according to the kind and thickness of the fish. The water should be lightly salted and 2 or 3 peppercorns and a bay leaf may be added for flavour if desired.

After the water has come to the boil the heat should be reduced till water has reached simmering (or poaching) point.

May be served with garnish, etc., as steamed fish.

Poached Fish
As boiled.

Grilled Fish
Lightly oil bottom of grill pan. Lay in the fish, sprinkle with salt and pepper. Rub lightly with oil or fat. Grill should be very hot. Small fish or fillets will take from 5-10 minutes. Turn unless very thin. Thick fillets or whole fish should be placed at low position in the grill. Small whole fish will cook better and more evenly if they are cut across with deep gashes.

Scalloped Fish
For this scallop shells (well-washed) are used. Take about $\frac{1}{2}$ lb (225 g) of a white fish and poach in skim milk. A little lemon juice, white wine, or bay leaf may be added if desired. After the fish is cooked, strain off the liquor to serve as a basis for sauce. Place the fish in 2 scallop shells, pour the sauce over them.

Roll bread-crumbs in about 1 teaspoonful of cooking oil. Sprinkle these over the fish and brown under the grill. A little potato, creamed with skimmed milk, may be used as a border.

Fish Curry
A way of using up left-overs of cooked fish. Remove all bones and break the fish into small pieces. Slice a small onion into thin strips (cut lengthwise) brown in a little oil or butter. Add 1 cup of hot skim milk and 1

teaspoonful curry powder. Mix 1 teaspoonful flour into a smooth paste with a little cold water, add gradually about $\frac{1}{2}$ cup of hot liquid from the frying pan. Return to frying pan, stir in the flour mixture very slowly. Add fish pieces, cover pan, and warm through on low heat.

Creamed Fish
Left-over cooked fish may be heated between plates, over steam, then served with white or brown sauce, plain or with parsley or other herbs.

SAUCES

White Sauces

(a) Thin sauce: 1 tablespoonful whole meal flour, 1 teaspoonful vegetable oil, 1 cup skim milk, $\frac{1}{2}$ teaspoonful sea salt.

(b) Medium sauce: As above, except 2 tablespoonsful flour.

(c) Thick sauce: As above, except 3 tablespoonsful flour.

Method: Bring the flour to a smooth paste by mixing with some of the milk. Add the oil, salt, and remaining milk. Bring to boiling point over moderate heat, stirring constantly. Remove from fire as soon as it begins to bubble. (Can be made without butter.)

Onion Sauce

several small onions or a handful of shallots
sea salt
white sauce

Cover the onions or shallots with boiling water, add salt, and boil for half hour. Drain and push through a sieve. Add to white sauce, having $\frac{1}{2}$ cup onion *purée* to 1 cup of sauce.

Bread Sauce

Cook 1 medium-sized onion in 2 cups of skim milk, very slowly. Season with salt and pepper and add whole meal bread-crumbs. Beat in thoroughly and serve.

To be served with poultry or game.

Tartare Sauce (fatless)

Put in a bowl 2 tablespoonsful each of Worcester sauce and vinegar, 1 tablespoonful lemon juice, $\frac{1}{2}$ teaspoonful sea salt, and 6 tablespoonsful of water. Set in a pan of hot water to heat through.

To be served hot with fish.

Mint Sauce

1 tablespoonful brown sugar or honey, $\frac{1}{2}$ tablespoonful cider vinegar, $\frac{1}{2}$ cup water, 2 tablespoonsful of mint, chopped finely. Should stand for at least $\frac{1}{2}$ hour before serving.

Horseradish Sauce

To 1 cup medium white sauce add 3 tablespoonsful horseradish. Allow to cool.

MEATS

Grilled or Broiled Steak
The best cuts of beef for this are sirloin, crosscut of rump, and second and third cuts from the top of the round. Steak can be grilled with very little oil. Place the meat under a very hot grill and turn frequently, for 5-8 minutes, according to thickness and degree of rareness required. It is seldom necessary to pound or marinade steak if it is cooked in this way.

Grilled Bacon and Tomatoes
Place lean bacon under a medium hot grill. Cook until done. Keep warm. Cut tomatoes into thick slices, place under grill and heat through. This will only take about 5 minutes.

Steak Casserole
8 oz (225 g) very lean rump steak
1 carrot, grated
1 chopped onion
seasoning
2 teaspoonsful tomato sauce or *purée*
jellied stock or liquid
1 stick of celery, chopped
garlic if desired

This recipe can be halved or the quantity otherwise

adjusted according to need. Mix enough of the carrot and onion to blend with the tomato and a little stock. Season and mix thoroughly. Set aside. Place the celery and the remaining carrot and onion in a casserole.

Divide the meat into two thin pieces. Flatten them with a rolling pin or jar. Place half the filling which has been set aside on each piece. Roll up and pin with a skewer or tie with string. Rub with garlic if desired. Lay the meat in the casserole on top of the vegetables, add enough stock (or water) to cover, and simmer for 2-3 hours. If water is used it can be flavoured with yeast or beef extract. If a thick-bottomed pot is used, this dish can be cooked on top of the stove.

Lamb Casserole

1 lb (450 g) very lean stewing lamb
3 small carrots
2 or 3 slices of turnip
½ pint (275 ml) water
1 teaspoonful of yeast extract

Cut meat into small pieces. Cut carrots lengthwise and turnips into small pieces. Put all into a casserole, season with salt and pepper, herbs and garlic, as desired. Dissolve the yeast preparation in heated water and pour over casserole mixture. Cook in a moderate oven about 1½ hours. (If preferred this may be simmered gently on top of stove for 1-1½ hours, until almost cooked, then finished off under the grill).

Ham and Orange Casserole

2 thick slices of very lean ham
2 cloves
dash of made mustard
$\frac{1}{2}$ teaspoonful grated orange rind
1 tablespoonful honey
2 tablespoonsful orange juice
1 tablespoonful Barbados sugar

Insert a clove into each slice of ham and place in a casserole. Mix together the mustard, orange juice and rind, honey and sugar. Pour half of this over the meat, cover and bake in a moderate oven for $\frac{1}{2}$ hour. Add the rest of the mixture, and place dish for about 5 minutes, uncovered, under a hot grill.

Ham and Pineapple Casserole

As above, substituting pineapple for orange, in which case the cloves and mustard should be omitted.

Curry

$\frac{1}{2}$ lb (225 g) cooked meat, cubed
$\frac{1}{2}$ green pepper, chopped
2 tablespoonsful vegetable oil
1 teaspoonful tomato ketchup
brown rice (boiled)
1 medium onion
$\frac{1}{2}$ tablespoonful curry powder
$\frac{1}{2}$ cup stock
1 small teaspoonful cornflour
salt and pepper

Cook onion and pepper in oil until soft, add curry powder and cook for another 3 minutes. Stir in stock, meat and tomato. Bring to boil, cover and simmer for 10 minutes. Blend cornflour with 2 tablespoonsful stock and stir into curry. Stir until it thickens and season to taste. Flavour will be improved by addition during last 10 minutes of chopped apple, raisins or sultanas.

Mutton Ragout

$1\frac{1}{2}$ lb (675 g) lean neck of mutton
1 small onion
2 small carrots
2 teaspoonsful vegetable oil
$\frac{1}{2}$ pint (275 ml) hot water
2 small turnips
1 small clove garlic (or
    1 teaspoonful garlic salt
salt and pepper

Slice the mutton into cutlets. Dice the onion and carrots, peel the turnip and cut into thick slices. When the oil is hot in the saucepan, add the meat, carrots and onion. Sprinkle over them a little flour and stir until all are brown. Then add the hot water and seasoning. Cover, and simmer for about 1 hour. Add the turnip and continue simmering until meat and turnips are cooked.

Middle Eastern Dish

1 lb (450 g) cubed lean lamb or beef (raw)
1 lb (450 g) tomatoes
1 green pepper
1 lb (450 g) mushrooms
1 large onion
bay leaves

Marinade: 1 cup oil, garlic, sea salt, black pepper

Soak meat in marinade at least an hour before cooking. Remove stems from mushrooms, cut peppers and onions into cubes. Brush all vegetables lightly with oil. Arrange vegetables and meat alternately on skewers and broil quickly.

They can be served with brown rice or potatoes.

Cubes of fresh pineapple can be substituted for meat, in which case no marinade is needed.

Breast of Lamb (stuffed with brown rice)
Ask butcher to make a pocket in the breast of lamb for the stuffing. Trim fat from it and rub a cut clove of garlic inside and outside the meat.

¾ cup brown rice, parboiled 15 minutes in sea salted water
¼ cup chopped raw peanuts, pecans or any mixed nuts combination
4 tablespoonsful whole meal flour with added wheat germ and soya flour
2 tablespoonsful minced parsley
4 tablespoonsful vegetable oil
2 cups water or stock
seasoning

Combine drained rice, nuts and parsley. Fill pocket in breast of lamb and fasten opening with skewers or sew it with strong white thread. Rub in flour mix. Heat fat in roasting pan and place meat in centre, basting with some of the oil. Roast in a hot oven for 30-35 minutes per pound of meat, basting occasionally.

Scalloped Ham
8 oz (225 g) lean ham
1 lb (450 g) potatoes
1 medium onion
hot skim milk

Cut peeled potatoes into very thin slices and grate peeled onions. Slice ham into thin strips. Starting with potato and onion, place alternate layers in baking dish or casserole with layers of ham, seasoning each time, ending with potato. Pour hot milk over ingredients as far as top layer, but do not cover this. Bake, uncovered, in moderate oven, or under moderate grill until tender, approximately one hour in oven. If done under grill it would be advisable to pre-cook potatoes.

Grilled Cutlets

4 lamb cutlets (lean)
1½ tablespoonsful brown sugar
1 tablespoonful made mustard or 1 teaspoonful dry mustard
sea salt and pepper

Season cutlets with salt and pepper and spread both sides with mustard (if dry mustard used, make a paste with water). Dip in sugar. Grill under high setting, turning frequently. Cooking time will depend on thickness of the meat.

Mince Casserole

Brown ½ pound (225 g) of minced lean beef in a little melted butter. Add about ½ pound (225 g) tomatoes (tinned or fresh), salt and pepper, and a small teaspoonful of Worcester sauce. Bring to boil. In a casserole place in layers 2 thinly sliced medium potatoes, ½ cup finely sliced celery, a little sliced green pepper, a small sliced onion. Cover with the meat mixture and top with a layer of sliced potato. Cover and cook for about an hour in a medium oven.

COOKED MEAT DISHES

Meat Shape
1 cup cooked lean meat
1 cup mashed potato
salt and pepper
1 tablespoonful sago
2 tablespoonsful stock
1 tablespoonful chopped parsley

Soak sago in stock for one hour. Add all the other ingredients to the finely minced meat, mix thoroughly and knead together. Put into a greased basin, press well down, cover as in meat soufflé, and steam for about an hour. May be served hot or cold with salad.

Quick Hash
1 cup finely minced cold lean meat
1 small onion
handful of raisins
2 teaspoonsful vegetable oil
2 cups hot mashed potatoes
1 tablespoonful flour
½ pint (275 ml) stock or water
browning

Slice the onion lengthwise into very thin strips and fry in the oil until brown (for 'stir frying' see *Miscellaneous* at the end of the book). Add the stock or water. Mix the flour to a smooth paste with a little cold water and add to liquid in the pan, stirring until it has boiled. Simmer for about 3 minutes, season, colour with browning or yeast extract, add meat. When onions are cooked, pour the mixture into the middle of a dish and arrange mashed potatoes around the edge. Parsley may be used for a garnish and tomatoes, cut in wedges, also add to its appearance.

Pilaff

1 small onion
1 cup finely minced cooked lean meat
½ cup uncooked brown rice
1 cup tomatoes (tinned or fresh)
2 teaspoonsful vegetable oil
½ pint (275 ml) hot water

Fry the thinly sliced onion to a delicate brown in the oil. Add water, season with salt and pepper, add the rest of the ingredients, except meat. Cover the pan and cook over medium heat until the rice is done. Add more water if necessary to keep from scorching, but take care not to make mixture watery. Add the meat and heat through. A little cayenne or curry may be used.

Basic Curry

This can be used with cooked meat, fish, or vegetables.

1 tablespoonful flour
1 level dessertspoonful Indian curry powder
1 tomato
1 onion
large handful raisins
large handful chopped apple

1 dessertspoonful marmalade
1 dessertspoonful chutney
1 pint (275 ml) stock or water
1 dessertspoonful vegetable oil

Heat the oil in a pan and brown onion in it. Take out onion and put into saucepan or other cooking vessel large enough to take all ingredients. Mix curry powder and flour in 2 or 3 tablespoonsful cold water in the frying pan. Place over medium heat and add, very gradually, the remainder of the stock or water, stirring constantly until it boils. Care must be taken not to add the liquid too quickly or the flour-curry mixture will go into lumps. Pour into saucepan with the onion in it, add other ingredients and let simmer until the onion and apple are cooked. Season to taste.

Shepherd's Pie

cooked lean meat, about $\frac{3}{4}$ lb or 350 g
1 small onion
1 lb mashed (450 g) mashed potatoes
salt, pinch cayenne pepper
1 cup stock or water flavoured with yeast
    or meat extract

Peel and slice the onion, lengthwise, into thin strips. Trim fat or gristle from meat and mince. Add a little milk to the potato and beat until it is smooth and fluffy. Put a layer of potatoes into an oiled casserole. Add meat, onion and seasoning. Pour in sufficient liquid to moisten, and cover with remaining potato. Rough up with a fork and heat in a hot oven for about $\frac{1}{2}$ hour.

Curry Pie

Use basic shepherd's pie recipe.

Mix 1 teaspoonful curry powder to a paste in a little cold water and add this, with a dessertspoonful of chutney, to the liquid to be used in the shepherd's pie. A layer of sliced apple may also be added before the second layer of potato.

Stuffed Marrow
Wash the marrow and split in two lengthwise, if it is a large one. If the marrow is small remove a wedge from the top. Scrape out the seeds and make a space for the filling.

Filling 1: Minced lean ham, mixed with chopped tomatoes and herbs, and a little tomato ketchup to moisten, salt and pepper.

Filling 2: Bread-crumbs, mixed with finely chopped onions, minced lean beef (cooked or raw) moistened with stock and seasoning.

Filling 3: As 2, with any cooked lean meat.

Filling 4: Minced or diced cooked lean meat, grated onion, parsley, $\frac{1}{2}$ teaspoonful dry mustard, 4 tablespoonsful bread-crumbs, salt, pinch of cayenne pepper, milk enough to bind together.

These are only suggestions. Many other combinations or materials may be used also. (Where onions are used, unless grated, it is advisable to parboil them for five to seven minutes.)

Stuff the marrow, put halves together, or replace wedge, tying with string. The marrow may then be wrapped in greaseproof paper and steamed for approximately $1\frac{1}{2}$-2 hours, or in a greased pan in a hot oven.

Stuffed Peppers

After cutting the tops and stems from the peppers, remove the seeds and fibres and slice endwise through the middle. Parboil in salted water for five minutes.

Use any filling desired, e.g., those listed above, and fill the peppers to within $\frac{1}{2}$ inch of the top. Sprinkle with breadcrumbs, place in baking dish containing hot water. Bake in a hot oven for 40-60 minutes, until peppers are tender.

Beef Casserole

1 cup cold lean beef cut into cubes
2 teaspoonsful Worcester sauce
2 teaspoonsful tomato ketchup
1 small onion, thinly sliced from top to bottom
$\frac{1}{2}$ teaspoonful dry mustard

Put the beef into a greased, shallow baking dish. Combine the other ingredients and pour over meat, keeping back a little onion. Add enough water to cover and bake in a moderate oven for about 1 hour. Garnish with onion.

Sour Apple Casserole

1 cup diced or sliced cold lean meat
1 medium onion, sliced
2 teaspoonsful melted butter
salt and pepper
pinch of nutmeg
1 large peeled and sliced sour apple
2 or 3 sliced, boiled potatoes
$1\frac{1}{2}$ cups (approximately) stock or water flavoured with yeast extract

Brown onions and apples lightly in the hot fat. Into a greased baking dish place alternate layers of onions, apples and meat. Pour over enough stock to cover. Add nutmeg, salt and pepper. Bake in moderate oven for about 45 minutes.

SALADS

In the Bircher-Benner clinic results have proved over the years the beneficial and curative effects of eating raw foods every day, *particularly at the beginning of each meal.*

A large number of chemical and physical properties, as yet hardly investigated, are altered by heat, and some important vitamins are lost. These are important for the healthy functioning of the endocrine gland, the mucous membrane, the blood vessels, the cell walls and the formation of the blood. Some of these functions could well be concerned in the handling of cholesterol by the body. Food that has to be cooked should always be steamed rather than boiled.

Vital enzymes are also affected by the cooking process. These are particularly necessary for the establishment of healthy conditions in the intestines, and the lack of them can lead to disease.

Green vegetables, particularly leafy green ones, consumed raw are a valuable source of fibre. However, for those unused to eating raw foods, it is best at first to avoid mixing them. Begin with one raw green vegetable and some baked or steamed potatoes in their skins. After about a week a small helping of another raw herb or vegetable could be introduced. In all cases salads ·must be masticated thoroughly if they are to be proprly digested, and they should not be eaten in a hurry.

Raw cabbage is a good substitute for lettuce and is easy to digest if finely shredded or grated. It should always be eaten in small quantities at a time. Other good salad greens, in season, are French endive, water cress, mustard and cress, borage (grows like a weed once started and is self-seeding), spring greens, curly kale, spinach, young (rounded variety) dandelion leaves, young tops of nettles and chicory.

Spring onions, chives, horseradish, parsley, mint, chervil, dill and fennel may also play their part in a salad.

Tomatoes, celery, red or green peppers, and cucumber add colour and variety to many salad combinations.

Apples, raisins, walnuts, hazelnuts, dates, sunflower or sesame seeds will blend with almost everything. Soya splits, lately on the market (see *Soya*) are a tasty and nutritious additon to any salad.

Hints

Tomatoes go further if cut in wedges from top to bottom, rather than in horizontal rounds. Flavour is improved by a dash of both salt and sugar on each piece.

Cucumber is best cut very thinly, and a sprinkle of salt on each slice will bring out the flavour. It will keep well if wrapped securely in greaseproof paper (not plastic) and stored in the refrigerator or in a cold larder.

Celery will keep fresh for days if the lower part of

the head or stick is resting in cold water. It does not keep well if wrapped up and placed in refrigerator.

Cabbage, lettuce and other greens keep fresh and crisp in the refrigerator if sprinkled lightly with water and then put into plastic bags.

To Curl Celery

Cut the stalks into 2 inch pieces. Make several cuts from each end to within $\frac{1}{2}$ inch of centre.

Place in cold water and let it curl.

Radish Roses

These are made by peeling the prepared radish in $\frac{1}{8}$ inch strips from top to $\frac{1}{4}$ inch of the stem.

Place in cold water to curl.

Main Ingredients

The main ingredients of a salad may be divided into the following types:

(1) Cold meats, cold fish (including certain shell fish), jellied meats.

(2) Cottage cheese, yogurt.

(3) Jellied fruits or vegetables, fruit.

Salad Suggestions

With meat, eggs, fish, cheese, or cottage cheese as main ingredient:

Apple, celery, and nuts (suitably chopped).

Apple, celery, and dates.

Apple, celery, and raisins.

Onion and carrot finely grated, mixed with coarsely grated apple.

Onion and carrot, mixed, finely grated; tomato and cucumber separately.

Tomatoes, green peppers and cucumber.

Radish, in combination with green onions, apples or other ingredients.

Lettuce or grated cabbage.

Beetroot, parsnip, or turnip may be grated when raw and used with any other ingredients desired. Cooked beetroot, diced, cold cooked peas and beans, or other cold, cooked vegetables, may also be used up in this way.

Cooked potatoes are useful, either diced, cold, or sliced thinly and crisped under a hot grill (no fat used).

Pickles are good for flavouring, herbs for garnishing and flavouring, used with discretion. Olives may also play their part.

Tomato Jelly Salad

1 tablespoonful gelatine
2 tablespoonsful cold water
2 cups tomato juice
½ teaspoonful celery salt
1 teaspoonful chopped onion.

Soak gelatine in cold water (or follow instructions given on packet). Simmer tomato juice, onion and seasoning together for 10-15 minutes. Strain and add gelatine. Turn into moulds or basin.

Jellied Chicken

1 cup diced cooked meat
1 cup chopped celery
2 tablespoonsful cold water
1 cup stock
1 tablespoonful gelatine
½ teaspoonful onion salt

Soak gelatine in cold water, add to boiling stock

along with seasoning. Remove from heat, add other ingredients and turn into mould.

Nut Galantine

1 cup whole wheat bread-crumbs
fresh or dried mint or parsley, chopped finely
2 small tomatoes
1 small shallot (finely grated)
1 cup milled walnuts or hazel nuts

Scald and peel the tomatoes, press through a sieve. Add the herbs and shallot, then the bread-crumbs and nuts. Mix well. If more moisture is needed in order to form it into a loaf, add a little stock or water. Turn the mixture into a small basin, press down, cover and put a weight on top. After two hours, turn out and slice. To be served with a salad.

Cottage Salad: 1

1 lb (450 g) cooked potatoes
½ lb (225 g) cottage cheese
1 tablespoonful chopped chives or tops of spring onions
1 teaspoonful prepared mustard
½ lb (225 g) tomatoes
½ small cucumber
salt and a dash of pepper

Mix and toss together in a large bowl the cheese, chives, mustard, salt and pepper. Cut tomatoes into thin rings and cucumber into thin slices. Place the tomatoes and cucumber, along with sliced potatoes, into another bowl, pour over them some dressing and toss well together. Take a large dish or platter and arrange lettuce leaves around the edge. Next in circle place the vegetable mixture, and finally, in the centre, the cheese mixture.

Cottage Salad: 2

Grate 2 or 3 small carrots and soak in orange juice. Add small pieces of orange and chopped walnuts or hazel nuts. Blend in finely chopped parsley. Place this mixture into the middle of a dish and surround it with fresh watercress, young dandelion greens, or whatever is in season. Put lettuce around the edges. Dot with spoonfuls of cottage cheese, cubes of cooked potato or apples dipped in honey, or yogurt.

Artichoke Salad

Grate about a cupful of root artichoke, also a cup of cabbage. Arrange these on a plate, with a heap of grated raw carrot in the centre. Strew a few sprigs of watercress around the edges, and garnish with chopped parsley.

Nasturtium Salad

Shred lettuce leaves and heap in centre of plate. Grate raw carrot and raw beetroot (about $\frac{1}{2}$ cup each), mix together and arrange this around the lettuce. Cut 2 or 3 small tomatoes into wedges and arrange outside the other ingredients. Place nasturtium leaves around outside, together with a few spring onions, and decorate with nasturtium flowers.

Nasturtiums are a rich source of vitamin C.

SALAD DRESSINGS

Some Simple Dressings

1 teaspoonful of sunflower seed oil, safflower seed oil, olive or corn oil mixed with 1 cup fruit juice. Heat slightly to blend, then cool. Add a little lemon juice.

Honey, cider vinegar, and skim milk. Mix about a dessertspoonful of honey with enough warm water to dissolve it. Add 2-3 tablespoonsful cider vinegar, then about $\frac{1}{2}$ cup of milk. Shake well. This will look curdled but the taste is not affected, and it will keep for several weeks in refrigerator.

Yogurt mixed with honey makes a delicious salad dressing. May be mixed with chopped chives, parsley, mint, marjoram, finely grated onion, or paprika.

Mix the following ingredients in the proportions needed.

$\frac{1}{2}$ tablespoonful apple cider vinegar
3 tablespoonsful lemon juice
1 teaspoonful brown sugar
$\frac{1}{4}$ teaspoonful sea salt, a little pepper, a pinch of dry mustard, a little garlic or other herbs

---

1 tablespoonful cider vinegar
6 tablespoonsful water

1 teaspoonful oil
a little caraway seed powder
sea salt
grated onion

Soya Salad Dressing

3 tablespoonsful soya flour
3 dessertspoonsful dried skim milk
1 cup cold water or vegetable stock
1 dessertspoonful chopped chives
1 dessertspoonful chopped mint or tarragon

Mix soya flour and milk, add chives and other ingredients. Mix carefully with the cold liquid and stir over a low heat for 10-15 minutes. When cold add a dash of paprika. If no dried milk is at hand use ordinary milk instead of the cold water or stock.

Salad Cream

1 tablespoonful soya flour
1 dessertspoonful dried skim milk
cider vinegar
$\frac{1}{4}$ teaspoonful mustard
$\frac{1}{4}$ teaspoonful sea salt

Mix all dry ingredients to a paste with water. Add vinegar to thin out and to desired taste.

JELLIES

Agar-Agar
This is a natural jellying agent derived from seaweed, and is a complete substitute for gelatine. It is odourless, flavourless, and clear. Fruit or vegetable juices can be jellied with it without heating beyond blood heat, thus retaining most of their nutritional values. It is superior to commercially manufactured and processed jellies and gelatines, in that it contains no chemical or synthetic additives, nor need it be heavily saturated with white sugar, as in the case of so-called 'fruit' jellies sold under various brand names. Varieties of agar-agar can be obtained in health shops. With it many delicious fruit desserts can be made.

Apple Fluff
Prepare and stew apples, sweetened with a little brown sugar, to measure 1 pint. Mix 2 teaspoonsful of agar-agar to a smooth paste with a little cold water. Add the apples to this, stirring constantly. When the mixture boils let it cook for three minutes. Remove from heat and when it has cooled slightly add the grated rind of a lemon. Stir again and pour into moulds. Sets in 2-3 hours.

Fruit Jelly

This can be made with agar-agar, according to taste and fruit to hand, using 1 pint (550 ml) liquid to 2 teaspoonsful of agar-agar.

In all cases agar-agar must be mixed to a smooth paste in cold liquid.

FRUIT

Apples (for the role of apple in cholesterol control see section on Pectin in *Supplements*.)

Apple Purée
This can form the basis of many desserts. It is most appetizing and nutritious if nothing is cut away from the apple but the stem and any damaged parts. The core and pips contain valuable substances which investigators have found to have some function in promoting the health of the heart. However, in retaining the skin, there is of course a risk if it is not known whether the apples are sprayed. If the apples are too perfect and without blemishes (as in the case of other fruits and vegetables), heavy spraying must be suspected. Insects are too wise to go near them!

First wash the apples, remove stems and blemished parts, cut the rest into small pieces and put into a pan with about half as much water as apples. Stew slowly until the apples are soft. Remove from heat and rub through a sieve or purée in a liquidizer. The pulp will keep for several weeks in a jar in the refrigerator.

Bottled Apple Purée
If the puréed apple is put into a jar, with top

loosened, and heated slowly through in a moderate oven or up to the neck in hot water for 10-15 minutes, then removed and the top pressed down very firmly to exclude all air, it should keep indefinitely. When the top will no longer move at a touch, the jar will be sealed. It is necessary to have the jar filled to overflowing. The screw top jars now in the shops containing marmalade, jams, etc. will work admirably for this purpose. The apple should be sweetened at time of using if necessary.

Another method of bottling which is perhaps more reliable is to bring the purée to the boil in a saucepan, transfer it immediately to heated jars, (filled to the top), then quickly screw on top which has been sterilized in boiling water. This is very suitable for doing small amounts of any fruit at a time.

Apple Charlotte
Put apple purée into a shallow baking dish. Cover with brown or Barbados sugar, add a little cinnamon if desired. Sprinkle breadcrumbs or cornflakes over the top and add a few bits of butter and a little more sugar. Heat through under a moderate grill.

Apple Snow
Sweeten the purée with honey or brown sugar, add a little lemon juice and fold into it stiffly beaten egg white in the proportion of one egg white to one cup of purée.

Raw Apple Sauce
2 cups apples, quartered and cored (leave the skins on if they are organic)

½ cup raisins (unsulphured)
pinch of cinnamon
honey, if apples are tart

Put ¼ cup of water, or unsweetened pineapple or apple juice, in the blender, add the apples and reduce to a pulp. (Or put through a sieve or mouli). Add raisins and cinnamon and run for another minute. Add honey to taste, if needed. This apple sauce can be made when the apples are fresh and kept frozen for the winter.

Stewed Apples
Peel and core the apples. Cut into small pieces and cover with dark brown sugar. Add a few teaspoonsful of water and cook very slowly in a shallow dish, in oven, on top of stove, or under grill. Two or three cloves may be added.

Avocados
These are highly nutritious and will mix with almost any other fruit. One way in which they can be used is to cut them in half lengthwise and remove skin. Cut into cubes. Roll first in lemon juice, then in sesame seeds or ground nuts. Serve on toothpicks as a wholesome snack, which children especially like.

Tinned Fruit Purée
Tinned infant foods make an excellent base for puddings.

Dried Apples or Apricots
Wash with hot water. Soak overnight in clean, cold water. Simmer slowly until soft, and use as desired. Are suitable for all above recipes.

Baked Apples

Wash and core apples. Mix together chopped blanched almonds, raisins, and enough rose hip syrup to hold together. Stuff the apples with this mixture and bake in a fairly hot oven for 20-30 minutes, having a little water in the bottom of the dish.

Apple Meringue

Fresh apples, prepared for stewing, or dried ones soaked overnight may be used for this. Cook them in a little water until very soft. Then beat well, sweeten to taste with honey or dark brown sugar. Remove to a casserole. Whisk the whites of 2 eggs until stiff and dry, adding a little brown sugar. Pile on top of the apple, and heat in a moderate oven until brown.

Sponge Trifle

Break sponge cake into small pieces. Pour over it about 2 tablespoonsful of cooking sherry per person. Add custard, either liquid or whipped. Top with a little cooked fruit or jam. For best results this should be prepared about an hour before eating. It is a cook's way of using up stale cake.

Stewed Rhubarb

The flavour of rhubarb is greatly improved if it is cooked very slowly, either in the oven or on top of the stove, in its own juice. No water should be used, only brown or Barbados sugar to taste. The cooking process must be very slow or the rhubarb will burn.

PUDDINGS

Bread Pudding (baked)

4 slices bread, preferably whole wheat
1 tablespoonful currants, washed
1 tablespoonful sultanas, washed
1 egg
$\frac{1}{2}$ cup brown sugar
$\frac{1}{4}$ pint (150 ml) skim milk
1 tablespoonful vegetable oil
$\frac{1}{2}$ teaspoonful cinnamon
a few chopped almonds

Crumble the bread and soak it in the milk for about 1 hour. Add the fruit, cinnamon, sugar and nuts. Use part of the butter to grease a dish or casserole. Add the rest of it to the other ingredients, mixing well. Lastly stir in the well beaten egg. Bake in a moderate oven for 1 hour. The sugar may be omitted if preferred.

Bread Pudding (steamed)

2 cups breadcrumbs
1 cup hot water
$\frac{1}{2}$ teaspoonful bicarbonate of soda
1 egg
$\frac{1}{4}$ teaspoonful ground ginger
3 tablespoonsful molasses
    or treacle

1 cup whole wheat flour
1 cup raisins
1 tablespoonful vegetable oil
$\frac{1}{4}$ teaspoonful ground cinnamon
A little milk if the mixture is too stiff.

Dissolve the molasses or treacle in the hot water, add soda, and pour over the breadcrumbs. Let mixture soak for about $\frac{1}{2}$ hour. Add raisins, melted butter and beaten egg. Sift flour and spices together and blend into the rest of the mixture, adding skim milk if necessary. Steam $1\frac{1}{2}$-2 hours.

Shredded Wheat Pudding
To every shredded wheat biscuit add 2 cups hot milk, 1 egg, $\frac{1}{3}$ cup molasses or treacle, $\frac{1}{2}$ teaspoonful salt, $\frac{1}{2}$ teaspoonful ground cinnamon or ginger. Pour over biscuits and bake in a moderate oven until set – about $\frac{1}{2}$ hour.

Steamed Pudding (with soya flour)
3 tablespoonful, rounded, self-raising whole wheat flour
1 rounded tablespoonful soya flour
2 good tablespoonsful polyunsaturated margarine
1-2 tablespoonsful brown sugar
Milk, or milk and water, or water, to mix

Sift all dry ingredients, and rub in fat. Mix to a soft dough with liquid. Put in an oiled basin and steam for 1 hour.

Variations on Steamed Pudding
Ginger Pudding Add 1 teaspoonful ginger and 1 dessertspoonful syrup.
Marmalade Pudding Omit sugar. Put 1 tablespoonful marmalade in the bottom of the pudding basin before adding the mixture.

Soya Crispie

1 lb (450 g) stewed apples, sweetened
2 dessertspoonsful flour
1 dessertspoonful brown sugar
1 dessertspoonful soya flour
1 oz (25 g) polyunsaturated margarine

Rub fat into mixed flours. Add sugar and sprinkle this dry mixture on top of apples in a shallow dish. Bake in a moderate oven until biscuit coloured, or heat under a moderate grill.

NUTS AND SEEDS

Nuts are storehouses of protein, fat, vitamins, minerals, trace elements and carbohydrates, each variety providing different combinations of these substances. They have a high nutritional value and should only be eaten a few at a time. If they are not chewed slowly and carefully they can be indigestible. Their natural fat does not have the tendency to build up cholesterol in the body, since nuts are a whole food with a proper balance of constituents.

One of the most valuable properties of nuts is that most of them contain good proportions of the B vitamins, which are so necessary to health and so scarce in modern diets, along with equally scarce minerals and trace elements, such as zinc and chromium. Scientists are now discovering that both of these trace elements have a very important part to play in nutrition.

The nuts containing most fat are pecan, hickory, filbert, Brazil, beechnut, walnut and coconut. Almonds are high in protein, B vitamins, minerals and trace elements. Chestnuts are low in protein, high in carbohydrates, the B vitamins, minerals and trace elements. Peanuts are high in protein, medium high in fat, high in B vitamins, minerals and trace elements – one of the best balanced and most nutritious nuts there is, though perhaps not as good as either sunflower or sesame seeds. The English walnut also ranks high nutritionally.

For those faced with the necessity of eating processed foods every day, eating seeds can be a wonderful source of protection, particularly during those seasons when stored vegetables and fruits have lost so much of their nutritional value. One of the great advantages of eating raw seeds is that they contain good proportions of natural unsaturated fatty acids. Apart from this, experiments have shown that the seed will absorb very little of the inorganic fertilizers and pesticides which are taken up by the rest of the plant. Nature will reject what is not suitable for the propagation of the species.

Sunflower Seeds

The sunflower, which worships the sun all day, is one of the few plants which provides vitamin D. This helps in the utilization of calcium and phosphorus, which are in plentiful supply in this seed. The fat-soluble vitamins A and K are also present, along with a high content of the B vitamins and vitamin E, all of which are especially good for the heart and blood vessels.

Sunflower seeds are 24 per cent protein and contain every essential amino acid in a good balance. These power-houses of nutrition are also rich in minerals and trace elements, including iodine. One of their most valuable components is potassium (they are high in potassium and low in sodium, i.e. salt). Potassium is a mineral vital to heart function. Sodium, so often used in excess in the modern diet, is an enemy of potassium and contributes greatly to hypertension and overweight.

Sesame Seeds

These can be compared in many respects with sunflower seeds.

NB: $\frac{1}{8}$ to $\frac{1}{4}$ pound (about 50-100 g) are suggested daily amounts of seeds for one person, though other foods consumed during the day, or with them, must be taken into consideration. All nuts and seeds are highly concentrated foods.

Sprouting Seeds

It is said that nearly three quarters of the world's food supply is now in the form of seeds – the grains, such as wheat, rye, barley, rice, millet, and the pulses or legume family which include peas, beans and lentils.

A seed is a veritable power-house of energy, for in its natural state it contains all that is necessary to bring the plant life and sustain it during its germination period. When seeds are sprouted and used as food (which the Chinese have done for thousands of years) there may be some loss in protein, but scientists have found that there are big gains in other nutrients. The sprouts retain the B complex vitamins present in the original seeds and show a great increase in the amounts of vitamins A and C. It has been found that a cup of almost any sprouted seed provides as much vitamin C as 12 glasses of orange juice. Another result of the sprouting process is that starches are converted to simple sugars, thus aiding digestion of the seeds.

A word of caution about the use of seeds for sprouting – it is wiser, if possible, to obtain seeds which have not been treated by chemicals such as those used by many seed producers. Several seed houses will provide untreated seeds for sprouting, and some varieties can also be found at health stores.

Though apparently expensive to buy, the nutritional value of the sprouts is so high that a teaspoon or two at a time, along with other foods, is quite sufficient. Also, the yield of sprouts to original seed is increased in bulk to about 4 cups to 1, including husks, which in some cases can be eaten.

To obtain the greatest food value the sprouts should be eaten raw, but they can be cooked, by stir frying or boiling in just enough water to cover them, over a slow heat.

To Sprout Seeds

The simplest and easiest way is to pierce the top of a screw top jar, making holes which are large enough to let water run out yet small enough to keep the seeds in. The seeds used should fill no more than a $\frac{1}{4}$-$\frac{1}{2}$ the jar, as they will swell to several times their original size. Add water, screw on top and shake well, so that all the seeds are moistened. Hold jar upside down and let all surplus water flow out. Put jar on its side and roll about to separate seeds as much as possible. Keeping jar on its side, wrap around it a thick towel or piece of cloth to keep the seeds in darkness, and let it stay in this position at room temperature. Ideally, the seeds should be rinsed and restored to darkness several times a day, but I have experienced no difficulty when only rinsing once or twice daily.

In many seeds the outer husk or case will gradually loosen during sprouting and may float away in the rinsing process. If not, it will be necessary in the case of the harder seeds, such as legumes, to separate the sprouts from the husks when the sprouting process is complete.

Cereal and grain sprouts, including alfalfa, may be improved by a few hours in artificial light, or indirect sunlight, to let them develop chlorophyll. This is called 'greening' and which gives them a slightly sweet, fresh-green taste. A sprout length of 1-2 inches is generally best for this process.

Some seeds will sprout in 2 or 3 days, others will take up to a week. The sprouts should be used when they reach the same length as the original seed. If a larger quantity is made than can be eaten within 24 hours, they can be put into the freezer or freezing compartment of a refrigerator, where they will keep for a week or more. Or they may be dried for a few minutes in the oven (at about 350°, gas mark 4) with the door open or under the grill. Spread out evenly in either case, and stir at intervals. After the drying process they can be crushed to a fine powder and stored in a jar.

As well as being eaten raw, or cooked as previously suggested, sprouts, whether frozen or dried, can be added to soups, breads, cakes in fact, to almost any food.

One of the most nutritious of the sprouts is alfalfa, which is packed full of vitamins, minerals and trace elements in forms the body can easily assimilate. There is also an exceedingly high protein content.

The most usual seeds for sprouting are the

different varieties of beans, including soy, and they are all good. The seeds of cauliflower and other brassicas will sprout, but become strong in flavour if allowed to grow too long. Peas are good. Sunflower and sesame seeds will sprout but tend to become bitter. Grains like wheat, rye and rice are often used.

Fenugreek is a tiny seed of the legume family. It sprouts very quickly, usually within 48 hours and can be eaten husk and all. It freezes well and is an excellent remedy for catarrh. Often it is combined with garlic to help in chest or throat disorders.

Several sproutings kits are now on the market, details of which can be found in health magazine advertisements.

CULTURED MILKS

Lactobacillus acidophilus
This is a fermenting bacteria used to prepare cultured milk, like buttermilk or sour milk. A small amount added to yogurt can increase its effectiveness, particularly in cases of colitis, indigestion or diarrhoea. *Lactobacillus acidophilus* is recommended for anyone facing surgery and for those with skin trouble. It is a natural gastro-intestinal antibiotic and will restore healing bacteria which have been destroyed by the use of drugs.

Pectin encourages the growth of *Lactobacillus acidophilus*. Sunflower seeds or apples are full of pectin and will help to keep the benign bacteria alive in the system. It is not recommended that this milk be taken regularly, only periodically, for a week or two at a time.

Sour Milk
Sour milk is a great aid to the digestion and very pleasant when eaten with fruit and a little sugar. My experience has been that it is often possible to sour ordinary milk from the dairies, though a little yogurt will be of help at times when there is no sour milk at hand to start the turning process.

The milk should be placed in a shallow basin and stood at ordinary room temperature for up to 48 hours, though with the aid of the yogurt or sour milk culture it will sour in about 24 hours. While souring, as in the case of yogurt, the container should not be disturbed.

Yogurt

Yogurt supplies milk protein to the body and is an aid to digestion. The bacteria it contains convert the lactose in milk to lactic acid and this supplements the action of hydrochloric acid in the stomach which is so necessary to digestion, particularly in the case of elderly people. It is also useful in combating the effects of antibiotics, such as penicillin. A team at Vanderbilt University discovered that yogurt tends to reduce cholesterol levels in the blood. Another of the characteristics of yogurt is that it promotes a healthy acid atmosphere in the intestines, which is helpful to the growth of *lactobacillus acidophilus*.

Making Yogurt

When making yogurt it is important to have a good culture to start off with. Once a batch is made, a few tablespoonsful from it will start another batch, though this should generally be renewed at least every 6-8 weeks. Sometimes the plain yogurt obtainable in grocery shops can be used with success, but the live culture in powdered form is very reliable and can be kept for several months.

Method
Bring 1 pint of milk to boiling point. Pour it into a basin and stand the basin in cold water to cool off.

When the milk has reached a lukewarm temperature, add 2 or 3 tablespoonsful of plain yogurt, or $\frac{1}{2}$ packet of dried culture. Stir briskly. Pour the milk into jars (it works best in two jars rather than one). Set the jars up to their necks in a bowl of lukewarm water, leaving the water level several inches below the top so that warm water can be added later if necessary. Wrap the bowl in a heavy towel or cloth to keep the water warm. Alternatively, set the water container over a very low heat or to the side of a plate or burner, with the heat turned as low as possible. The milk must never get above blood heat, and must not be disturbed or stirred. Using commercial yogurt the thickening process should take 3-5 hours. The powdered culture will initially take at least 8 hours, subsequently only $2\frac{1}{2}$ or 3 hours.

Soy Yogurt

Blend 1 pint of milk with 3 tablespoonsful soya flour. Bring to boiling point, then cool until lukewarm. Put 4 or 5 tablespoonsful of yogurt culture into the milk and mix well. Pour into prewarmed cups, glasses or jars (no larger than an ordinary cup (and put these into a bowl of lukewarm water which comes to the necks of the containers. Wrap with a heavy towel to conserve heat, and if the water cools add a little hot water without disturbing containers. The alternative method described above can also be used. After some hours the yogurt should be about the consistency of thick cream. Refrigerate and save part of the batch to start the next one.

CHEESE

Other than cottage cheeses, cheese should be avoided, one reason being that most varieties have a high salt content, known to affect the blood pressure. Processed cheeses are a product of doubtful value, since the original materials are put through several extra processing steps and can have additives of all descriptions incorporated in them, including dyes. It would take up too much space to list even a fraction of the additives here, but the rather frightening query emerges – as it does when doctors prescribe many different pills or capsules daily for one patient – what is happening to our metabolic functions when all these foreign substances are jumbled up together in it? Therefore I will repeat my advice to avoid processed foods, since they are often harmful.

Cottage Cheese
Since the commercial cottage cheeses contain chemical additives, used in the process of washing the curd, for flavouring, as preservatives or for other purposes, it does seem preferable to make your own if possible.

The method of making cottage cheese is to place

yogurt, *Lactobacillus acidophilus*, or soured milk
into a basin and set it over hot water for a few
minutes, so that the whey will separate from the
curds. When this has taken place pass the contents of
the basin through a muslin bag, allowing it to drip
until dry. What remains in the bag is then cottage
cheese, which can be seasoned to taste.

Low Acid Cottage Cheese

Into 2 pints of milk put a small piece of junket or
rennet tablet which has been dissolved in warm
milk. Heat the milk to about 90°F or 32°C (slightly
under lukewarm). Add acidophilus milk or yogurt.
Let it stand overnight, after which it should have the
consistency of firm yogurt. This is the curd. Break it
into small pieces and stand the bowl in a pan of
warm water. Leave the curd until it is heated to
about 110°F or 43°C (a thermometer is necessary for
this recipe). The bowl should be shaken occasionally
while it is heating, to distribute the heat evenly
through the curds. When the correct temperature is
reached turn off the heat and leave the bowl in the
water for about $\frac{1}{2}$ hour. The cheese can now be
placed in a muslin bag and hung where the whey can
drip into a bowl.

After the dripping process is completed the
cheese can be mashed with a fork. Other
flavourings, such as chives, a little sea salt or kelp,
can also be added.

Soya Cheese

This calls for 4 dessertspoonful soya flour, 2
dessertspoonful milk, and $\frac{1}{2}$ teaspoonful of yeast
extract. Heat the milk and dissolve yeast spread in it.

Blend this mixture slowly into the soya flour to make a thick paste, thinning with a little more milk if necessary. This may be flavoured with chopped chives or tomato.

Here is an alternative recipe which is equally good. 1 quart (1 litre) of soy milk, made from 6 tablespoonsful soya powder or soya flour blended into 2 pints of skim milk. Bring this to the boil. As it begins to rise, pour in $\frac{3}{4}$ tablespoonful of fresh lemon juice. Let stand until cold, then strain as in other cottage cheeses. Flavour to taste.

Whey

The liquid whey remaining in the basin after the making of cottage cheese is a very valuable food. It is the plasma part of the milk, i.e. whole milk modified by the lactic acid culture. It has an antiseptic action.

In dehydrated form whey has all the advantages of yogurt and the other lactic acid milks without any of the disadvantages of whole milk. When dehydrated without excess heat it contains 20 times the minerals of liquid milk and 50 times as much as lactose, or milk sugar, as yogurt or buttermilk. Lactose has the wonderful effect of combating any harmful intestinal flora.

SOYA PRODUCTS

Soya Flour

Soya flour contains about four times as much protein as cereals and twice as much as pulses. It is about 20 per cent fat. It contains no starch or sugar, but is rich in alkaline salts and essential vitamins. In South China soya is almost the only source of protein and is used widely in its natural state, the whole bean. Since soya in any form is such a concentrated food, being richer in fats and proteins than nuts and meat, it should be eaten only in small or moderate quantities at a time. It is particularly rich in lecithin and the important unsaturated fatty acids. It is also rich in the vitamins of the B group, in vitamin E and in mineral salts.

Soya flour can replace eggs, especially in pancakes or cakes, but only about a tablespoonful each time.

1 or 2 tablespoonsful of soya flour can be used with other flour to thicken soups, gravies or stews.

Soya Savory

Using 1 tablespoonful soya flour to 3 of mashed potato, blend together. Flavour with onion, chopped chives, parsley or other herbs and put into a greased dish. Heat through in oven or under grill until slightly browned.

Suggested proportions of soya flour to ordinary flour:

In cakes, pastries, yorkshire puddings, etc., 1 part of soya flour with 7 parts of cereal flour.

In steamed puddings, 1 part soya flour with 3 parts flour, but use a little extra baking powder.

There is now a product on the market called 'soya splits'. These are prepared from the soy bean, are slightly salted with sea salt and can be eaten like nuts. In appearance they resemble peanuts and are guaranteed free from chemical additives. They are delicious with salads or eaten as snacks. In our household we have been using about a tablespoonful each daily for the past 6 months and have noticed a great increase in our energy and vitality.

DRINKS

Milk Drinks

Tiger's Milk (An American drink).

3 level tablespoonsful powdered skim milk or soya flour to 1 pint (450 ml) of milk (or water for longer keeping). Add 2 teaspoonsful brewer's yeast powder and 2 or 3 tablespoonsful of blackcurrant or other strongly flavoured juice. Honey or black molasses may also be used.

Put the liquid into the bowl first, gradually adding dry ingredients, blending by hand or with an electric beater. Then add fruit juice. Molasses or honey will blend better if heated in a little skim milk or water. Wheat germ may also be added.

This may be stored in a cool place or in a refrigerator in a screw top jar. A few spoonsful added to hot milk makes a most beneficial drink.

Other Drinks

Put into a drinking glass a tablespoonful of blackcurrant or other fruit jelly. Leaving spoon in glass fill it with hot water and stir.

Add the juice of an orange and stir.

Parsley, when simmered, is a good remedial drink for kidney and bladder troubles.

Dried Fruit Drinks
Soak raisins, prunes, peaches or apricots in 4 times
their bulk of water for 48 hours. Simmer slowly until
soft, then press through a sieve or put in juicer. This
makes a healthy and pleasant drink.

BREADS

Bread-Making Hints

The tins should be warmed before the dough is put into them.

If the dough rises too high the loaf will be open and spongy and will dry out quickly; if it does not rise high enough the loaf will be too close and heavy. The proper amount of rising can be discovered by experience. When bread is cooked it will sound hollow when tapped with the knuckles. It should be turned out on a wire cooler and cooled quickly.

Wholemeal Bread

3 lb (1 k 350 g) whole wheat flour
2 pints (1 litre) water at blood heat
1 tablespoonful salt
1 tablespoonful Barbados sugar
1 oz. yeast.

Warm flour and baking tins. Mix the salt with the flour in a large basin and set over a very low heat to keep it warm. Crumble the yeast in a small basin, add sugar and a cup of warm water taken from the 2 pints. Leave this for 10 minutes to froth up, then stir to dissolve water. Stir with a wooden spoon until the flour is evenly wetted. Put the dough (which should be fairly wet) into the warm, greased tins, and place in a warm spot or in the oven at the lowest setting. Cover with a cloth and leave for about 20 minutes to rise by about a third, or until the dough is within an inch of the top of the tins. Bake in a moderate oven for about 40 minutes. Reduce heat if top becomes too brown.

Treacle Bread

4 oz (100 g) black treacle or molasses
2 eggs, well beaten
$\frac{1}{2}$ level teaspoonful baking powder
$\frac{1}{2}$ level teaspoonful bicarbonate of soda
2 oz (50 g) currants
2 oz (50 g) sultanas
$\frac{1}{4}$ pint (150 ml) milk
10 oz (275 g) whole meal flour
2 oz (50 g) margarine.

Put treacle (or molasses) and milk together in a saucepan and warm sufficiently for them to blend well. Turn into a basin and add eggs. Sift dry ingredients together and rub in fat. Add fruit and mix well, but do not beat. Bake in a well greased tin in a slow oven for 1-1$\frac{1}{4}$ hours.

Quick Bread

This recipe can also be used to make a dozen rolls.

4 cups flour (whole meal or mixed)
1 oz (25 g) fresh yeast (or 1 level tablespot ssl dried)
2 teaspoonsful sugar
2 teaspoonsful salt
$\frac{1}{2}$ pint water (lukewarm)

With fresh yeast: Rub yeast into flour, salt and sugar. Add this mixture to the warm water, and using one hand or a large wooden spoon mix to a soft dough.

Continue working it until it will leave the sides of the mixing basin, adding more flour if required.

With dried yeast: To 1 cup of the water add 1 teaspoonful of sugar, sprinkling the yeast on top. Let stand for about 10 minutes until frothy. Add this to the flour and remaining ingredients. Form into a dough and knead on a floured board.

For loaves: Half fill two well-greased baking tins with the dough, cover with a cloth or place inside a large greased polythene bag lightly tied and let rise to double original size. Remove covering and bake in middle of a hot oven for 30-40 minutes.

For rolls: Flatten prepared dough to $\frac{1}{2}$ inch thickness on floured board or table. Cut with $2\frac{1}{2}$ inch cutter or shape to half required size. Place on buttered baking sheet, leaving space for expansion, cover and let rise to double size. Bake at top of a hot oven for 20-30 minutes.

If a crusty finish is desired, brush tops with salt and water and sprinkle with cornflakes, baking 5 minutes longer. A crisp, light crust may be obtained by brushing with salad oil. A soft finish is obtained by putting rolls closer together on the baking sheet, brushing with milk and sprinkling with flour.

Apricot and Walnut Bread
This uses half the quantity of dough in above recipe. Work into the dough the following.

$\frac{1}{2}$ cup chopped dried apricots
$\frac{1}{2}$ cup chopped walnut meats
1 tablespoonful sugar
1 tablespoonful margarine

When the mixture is well blended turn it onto a floured board and shape so that it will fit into a 1 lb loaf tin. Follow instructions above for rising and baking.

Boston Brown Bread

1 cup corn meal
½ cup white flour
1 cup whole wheat flour
1½ teaspoonsful bicarbonate of soda
1 teaspoonful sea salt
2 cups sour skim milk
½ cup molasses or black treacle

Blend dry ingredients, mixing thoroughly. Add molasses and milk, heating slightly to blend if necessary. Turn into greased tins (e.g. empty soup tins) and steam for about 2 hours.

Potato Rolls

2 cups milk, scalded and cooled
4 small cooked potatoes, riced, kept warm
2 tablespoonsful molasses
1 tablespoonful dried yeast
1 tablespoonful polyunsaturated margarine
2 teaspoonsful sea salt

Add the yeast to a cup of the warm milk and the molasses. Let stand about 10 minutes until frothy. Other types of yeast may be used if the proper directions for them are followed. When the yeast mixture is ready add to it the potatoes, the rest of the milk, the fat and the salt, then enough flour to make a wet sponge. (Riced potatoes are made by putting cooked potatoes through a mill.) Cover and let rise in a warm place for about 1 hour, 2 hours at room temperature. If necessary, add more flour to make a dough dry enough to leave sides of mixing bowl. Knead, cover, and let rise again to double its bulk. Knead again and shape into balls. Place on an oiled baking sheet 1 inch apart, let rise, and bake 15-20 minutes in a hot oven, near the top.

Whole Wheat Scones

3 cups whole wheat flour
1 tablespoonful polyunsaturated margarine
2 tablespoonful sugar
1 egg
2 teaspoonsful baking powder
(or 1 teaspoonful bicarbonate of soda and 1 teaspoonful cream of tartar)
pinch of sea salt

Mix dry ingredients together. Rub in the fat, add egg and mix well with a fork. Add milk gradually, making a stiff dough. Roll out on a floured board to $\frac{3}{4}$ inch thickness. Cut with a cutter or form into shapes with hands. Place on an oiled baking sheet about 1 inch apart, brushing tops of rolls with milk. Bake near top of hot oven for 10-15 minutes.

HERBS AND SEASONINGS

A few herbs added to a recipe can much increase the zest and flavour of foods.

Chives and Parsley

Some of the well-known herbs, such as parsley and chives, can be used in many dishes. Parsley has for centuries been used as a medicine and one recent medical researcher, R.D. Pope, M.D., claims that it is 'excellent for the genito-urinary tract, of great assistance in the calculi of kidneys and bladder, albuminuria nephritis and other kidney troubles'. Some authorities also claim that it is an effective remedy, particularly when boiled with onions, for gall-stones.

Dried parsley may be used for flavouring or as a tea. Parsley, unlike many other herbs, will not dry if hung in the open air. Spread it out in a pan and place under a grill, medium heat, for 5-8 minutes, watching carefully to see it does not turn brown. It will then be possible to crush into a powder between the palms of the hands.

Garlic

May be obtained in several forms and must be used sparsely. Herbalists claim it is useful for respiratory affections.

Mint
For garnishing, or finely chopped as flavouring. Useful in soups or salads. For mint sauce, see *Sauces*.

Yeast Extract
There are several of these yeast-vegetable products available – all valuable for both flavouring and nutrition.

Paprika
A useful seasoning for fish, potatoes, vegetables, salads, some soups. May be used fairly generously.

Cayenne
A useful seasoning for soups, stews, meat dishes, salads, but only a pinch at a time.

SANDWICHES, SPREADS AND SAVOURIES

Simple Sandwich Fillings

Peanut butter on brown bread, with a little tart jelly spread over it, makes a nourishing sandwich which seems to have general appeal.

Salf-free yeast extract spread very thinly.
Cottage cheese with dandelion greens.
Soya cheese or savoury.
Cottage cheese with chopped apple.
Cottage cheese with chopped nuts.

Cottage Cheese Rolls

Cut crusts off bread, spread with cottage cheese, roll, and toast in the oven or under the grill.

Dr Rinse's Spread: 1

2 tablespoonful Rinse formula (see *Breakfast Dishes*)
1 tablespoonful safflower or other vegetable oil
1 tablespoonful brown sugar
1 tablespoonful peanut butter
2 teaspoonful boiling water

Mix the ingredients and spread on a slice of bread.

Dr Rinse's Spread: 2

2 tablespoonful Rinse formula
1 tablespoonful dark brown sugar
1 tablespoonful safflower or other vegetable oil
2 tablespoonsful peanut butter
2 tablespoonsful rolled oats

Mix above ingredients and spread on bread.

Avocado Spread

Mash together ripe banana and ripe avocado pulp. Add lemon juice and wheat germ, some sunflower seeds or chopped nuts.

SUPPLEMENTS

In view of the many environmental hazards today and the diversity of opinions among nutritionists, and in the scientific and medical world, about the needs of the body, I am giving below a few of the foods and food supplements which can help us to retain, or even regain, our health. Many of these supplements or foods can play a part in preventing the build-up of excess cholesterol in the blood or arterial systems.

Bran

Bran is much in the news today, even to the extent of being recommended by many members of the medical profession. The Scientific Council of the International Society for Research on Nutrition in its Resolution No. 38 stressed the importance of whole wheat bread for health. It had been found effective in lowering the blood cholesterol and forestalling vascular diseases. They placed particular emphasis on the vital importance of the crude fibre (unprocessed) bran on the outer layers of wheat and its ability to stimulate normal intestinal functions. This is also a powerful tool for the prevention of diseases such as diverticulitis, appendicitis and even bowel carcinoma, and many physicians are beginning to recognize this.

Brewer's Yeast

This contains sixteen of the twenty amino acids besides being a good source of almost all the known B vitamins, and the discovery was made in 1973 that this excellent food supplement also has a high chromium content. A lack of chromium intake has been found to produce faulty glucose metabolism, so that brewer's yeast can sometimes be useful in treating diabetes. Apart from this a chromium deficiency can cause the formation of fatty plaques in the arteries and this, of course, can lead to the build-up of excess cholesterol. In the case of diabetics this slowing up of the circulation often leads to gangrene and the cause of death in diabetic patients is frequently the closing off of arteries leading to the heart.

When starting to take brewer's yeast tablets, as with any other new food or food supplement, it is always as well to begin with very small quantities daily. In the case of yeast tablets start by taking only 1 or 2, always with meals. This amount can gradually be increased to a maximum of 8 daily. I have been taking 8 brewer's yeast tablets daily for the past 16 years and always notice a falling off in energy and general well-being if I keep off them for a few days. Also, within a week my eyes will begin to focus badly, tire quickly and become very sensitive to light.

Choline

This substance is a protector of the liver, that most

important gland in the body which regulates blood clotting, mineral balance in the tissues, elimination of toxic substances, the digestion of fats, and the release and storage of nutrients. The liver can become diseased when it is overloaded and overworked with too many fatty foods and is undernourished in the B-complex vitamin called choline.

Degenerative diseases, such as hardening of the arteries by deposited cholesterol, kidney lesions, liver cirrhosis, and muscular dystrophy have all been found to be reduced in animals eating diets high in choline. Choline enables the liver to burn up fatty acids.

Choline is abundant in, brown rice, wheat germ, brewer's yeast, soya beans and breast milk.

Kelp *(Seaweed)*
Kelp can be obtained in health stores in the form of powder or tablets. It is one of the richest sources known of vital minerals, approximately 30 in all, also of certain vitamins. It has been found to be helpful in treating indigestion and constipation, but results are only noticeable over a period of several months. Some people use it instead of salt, though this would be an acquired taste. Sea salt is also full of minerals and other nutrients not found in processed table salt.

Lecithin
One of the best emulsifiers known, i.e. it has the ability to break up globules of oil or fat so that the oil or fat can be more easily absorbed in the body. Lecithin can be obtained in the form of capsules at

health stores, and in foods is contained chiefly in egg yolks, liver and other organ meats, wheat germ, and all seed products, such as whole grains, sunflower seeds, lentils, soya beans, nuts. It is also a good source of phosphorus and the B vitamins.

But lecithin's most valuable function is its ability to process fats, so that instead of forming excess cholesterol throughout the body they are more easily absorbed into the system. Since gall-stones are largely and most often composed of cholesterol, lecithin can also help in the prevention of this disorder.

One woman who was using lecithin for the purpose of controlling cholesterol levels found to her astonishment that after 27 years of misery with migraine headaches these no longer occurred.

Molasses
This is a fine concentrated food, therefore not needed in large quantities at a time – only 1-3 tablespoonsful daily, and the blacker the better. The blacker the molasses, the more concentrated the iron, calcium, copper, magnesium, potassium and phosphorus content. It is very rich in the B complex, with the exception of vitamin B1 and folic acid, which are destroyed in the cooking process.

Olive Oil
The American Journal of Clinical Nutrition has stated that the taking of olive oil can effectively reduce blood cholesterol, and this has long been known to be helpful in getting rid of gall-stones.

In one article there is the report of studies at the French *Institut National d'Hygiene* in which a number of hospital patients suffering from high cholesterol levels were studied. After about four months, in patients taking as much olive oil as they wanted but no other oil or fat, the cholesterol levels were markedly lower. It could be that this cholesterol lowering ability of olive oil (unprocessed) is connected with the bile ducts.

Oatmeal

This cereal, that is the kind which needs cooking before use, loses less through milling processes than any of the others. It has one big drawback – it tends to rob the body of calcium. However, this can be overcome by the addition of milk or bone meal tablets. It is also important to take with it vitamin D in some form (perhaps fish liver oils) to help in the absorption of the calcium. Oatmeal is a good source of B vitamins, vitamin E, and several valuable minerals, particularly phosphorus.

Pectin

Recently the Department of Nutrition of Rutgers University announced that pectin, a carbohydrate found in the cell walls of many fruits and vegetables, may be an important factor in the prevention of heart disease. As far back as 1961, Dr Ancel Keys of the University of Minnesota stated that 'controlled experiments on man have shown that pectin in the diet has a small but definite effect on lowering blood cholesterol levels'. In experiments carried out on groups of middle-aged men in hospital the addition to the daily diet of 15 grammes (about $\frac{1}{2}$ oz) of pure pectin caused the blood cholesterol to fall by an average of about 5 per cent. When the pectin was removed from the diet the blood cholesterol promptly rose to the pre-pectin level.

Pectin is naturally contained in many fruits and berries, notably apples. To eat raw fruit (particularly after meals) would seem to be a way of getting pectin into the system far preferable to taking it in its pure state divorced from its components in the fruit or berry. At our present state of knowledge about nutrition, little is still known about the long term reaction of any 'pure' substance on the body, nor of the valuable minerals, vitamins and trace elements which may together ensure a proper balance which can be assimilated.

The old adage, 'An apple a day keeps the doctor away', could turn out to be a very true saying. The experiments at Rutgers have shown that pectin limits the amount of cholesterol the body can absorb.

In Italy they have found that uncooked apple sauce is bringing down cholesterol levels. An experiment with raw apples was conducted by three Italian doctors and the results were reported in a medical journal. Even after a high cholesterol diet tests showed that cholesterol levels went down when 2 or 3 apples in the form of blended or grated pulp were consumed after each meal. When the apple treatment was discontinued the cholesterol levels rose again.

Other known benefits of pectin (though not directly related to cholesterol control) are that it can prevent lead poisoning. The Russians claim that it can reduce the absorption and deposition of strontium 90 in the body. It is said by scientists at the Indiana University Medical Centre to be an effective germicidal agent which attacks both the staphylococci and streptococci organisms, and to provide an effective therapy for open wounds.

When eating apples with the skin on, if organically grown fruit is not available, the fruit can be washed in a solution of warm water and vinegar, then rinsed in clear water.

In oranges the pectins are present in the white membrane more than in the fruit itself. Other good sources of pectin are quince, bananas, avocados, cherries, currants, grapes, pineapples, raspberries, tomatoes, blackberries and peaches.

Rice Germ
Also a valuable source of nutritional substances.

Rutin
Found plentifully in buckwheat, rutin is a part of vitamin P (sometimes called a bioflavonoid). It generally appears in association with vitamin C. This vitamin has been found to be exceedingly useful in cases of high blood pressure, and other problems relating to the veins and arteries, including strokes.

Rose hips are especially rich both in vitamin C and the low flavoured Rose hip tablets or capsules can be obtained through health stores.

Vitamin C
In the United States, Dr Constance Leslie is convinced from her own experience and what she has observed from her patients that a long-term deficiency of vitamin C permits cholesterol to build up in the arterial system. She states: 'Science has known for years that vitamin C is essential for maintaining the smallest blood vessels, the

capillaries, and that bleeding from capillary breakage is the first overt sign of scurvy. I think we now have strong evidence that vitamin C is equally essential for the health of arteries and veins and that other diseases associated with these larger vessels can be caused by inadequate intake of vitamin C.'

Dr Constance Spittle, a pathologist at the Pinderfields Hospital, Wakefield, Yorkshire, believes that her investigations have proved that if there is enough vitamin C in the bloodstream to control fats the arteries will remain clean. By assisting in the transformation of cholesterol into bile acid, vitamin C lowers serum cholesterol levels, prevents the formation of plaques (of fat) and increases the production of bile acids. When the amount of bile is low, fats remain in such large particles that they cannot readily combine with enzymes, and consequently fat is not digested completely and its absorption is seriously hampered. This undigested fat can then become the source of many problems, including the forming of excess cholesterol and gall-stones, deep vein thrombosis and varicose veins.

Some investigators have found, when studying the nutritional habits of those who had suffered from coronary thrombosis, that there was a marked tendency towards a deficient intake of the B and C vitamins, in that all were predominantly white bread users and low in their use of fresh fruits and salads.

Vitamin E

Along with lecithin, vitamin E (another of the valuable nutrients removed from most breads) helps to prevent the oxidation of the fatty acids in the blood and increases oxygen available to the body tissues. The sad deficiency of this vitamin in our modern food is known to contribute greatly to the increase of cardiovascular problems, including the build-up of cholesterol, in the western world. Vitamin E is found chiefly in wheat germ, wheat germ oil, whole wheat and other whole grains.

Wheat Germ

This is sold in chemists or health stores. It contains not only high quality protein but good proportions of polyunsaturated oils. It also contains generous portions of vitamin E which helps to prevent the oils going rancid. Vitamin E is one of the best substances known to protect the heart and circulatory system. In fact, with the exceptions of vitamins A, C, and B12 there is present in wheat germ practically every nutrient known to be required by the body. Wheat germ oil has been found to be an effective controller of excess cholesterol in animals. It has also been known to aid women with a history of abortion to produce live children.

INDEX